C000256711

Becoming Unstuck

Your simple step by step guide to taking charge of your Life.

Written by Will Aylward

Will Aylward

ISBN:
9780463053614

DEDICATION

To the Warriors, those of us in life who get
back up and fight no matter how many times
they fall.

CONTENTS

Section Three

Moving forward

Section Four

Making it happen

Section Five

8 principles for becoming unstuck

Final thoughts

Introduction.

Whether you think you can, or you think you can't, either way you are right

- Henry Ford.

I'm a lover of quotes. For me, quotes are special. They remind us of core truths about who we really are and the true nature of this crazy thing we call life. When we read words that ring true for us, something inside just resonates, right?

Words are powerful.

We use words to describe ourselves and our experience of life. We use words to talk about who we think we are and who we think we're not. We experience words in the form of thought, the chattering between the ears that can be a blessing or a curse.

Words have the power to create and the power to destroy.

In the past, haven't words moved you to tears, in both a good and a bad way?

That's the power of words.

My intention is for the words contained between the pages in this book to remind you of some core truths about who you really are. It would bring a smile to my face if my words would bring clarity to you about; what you want, what might be holding you back and how you might move forward.

I'd love for my words to Inspire you. To reassure you. To contain ideas that will change your life, if only in a small way.

Who is this book for?

It must have been a couple of years ago when I first had this "absurd" thought.

I want to write a Book.

Although it would be two years later until I truly committed and made it happen, when this thought first came to me I did what many of us do when we want to learn how to do something we've never done before.

I popped "How to write a book" into google.

After scrolling through several articles, one tip kept popping up time and time again, so I figured it must be worth knowing.

The tip was this: be clear about WHO you are

writing your book for.

Made sense, I thought to myself. But in the beginning, I wasn't certain exactly who I was choosing to write this book for.

Then one day, it came to me... in the shower. Funny how great ideas and thoughts come to us in the shower, isn't it? I'm clear now I'm writing this book for two people...

You and Me.

Upon realising this, I said to myself "How can you be writing a book for yourself, Will"?

Then I got it. When I say I'm writing this book for me, more specifically it's for a *part* of me. You see, there's a small part of me, a whisper, which has convinced me I don't have what it takes to write a book. This whisper tells me I needn't bother because nobody is going to read it. It asks *Who do I think I am to write a Book*?

I know this whisper well. It's a whisper we all have, the voice of doubt and fear, who likes to stamp out the fires of our desires with *what ifs* and *yeah buts*.

Yeah but nobody will read your book.

What if it's a load of mumbo jumbo?

Yeah but... you've never written a book before?

Is this sounding familiar? I thought so.

As you'll come to learn, for years, this voice would dominate my life, keeping me stuck. Crippling me with anxiety, dread and a constant feeling of helplessness.

Not anymore. I've come to learn the voice of Doubt and Fear we live with is a **terrible** predictor of just what is possible for us in our lives. So rather than obey this voice, I **rebel** against it. When I hear a whisper saying *You can't do that, you're not good enough.* I respond with a playful "Let's just wait and see". I would go so far to say as it's our *duty* to challenge our fears and doubts and discover the boundaries of possibility for ourselves.

How come?

The unchallenged whispers become our truths.

I mean, if I had listened to the whisper saying *nobody will read your book* and not written this book then, obviously, nobody would have read the book! The unchallenged whisper would have become my truth. Not because the whisper reflected what is possible but simply because it would have gone unchallenged.

If you take away just one idea from this Book (I hope you don't because there's loads more powerful ideas to come) let it be this... Challenge your whispers!

That alone would be life changing. Imagine the changes, dreams and desires you'd make a reality.

Now, although I've come a long way since the days when this voice would dominate my life, the whisper is still there, lurking in the background like a hungry hyena.

That's why part of the reason I'm writing this book is to show this voice who is boss.

Although I may not know you, I know this about you. You have your own whispers. Your own *Gremlins* as I like to think of them, who like to convince you you're not powerful.

Let me start by saying this...

You are powerful. Beyond belief.

I'm curious, as you just read that, did you notice any Gremlins offer any commentary? Perhaps *Yeah, whatever* or *How does this schmuck know if I'm powerful or not?*

Whether you believe me or not, it's Ok for now because by the end of this Book my intention is to SHOW you. Seeing is believing, after all.

More importantly than me writing this book for a part of myself, I'm writing this book for you.

I'm writing this book for you if:

- Right now, you feel stuck, helpless or hopeless, like you're going around in circles, like your treading water but not going anywhere.

- You fantasize about turning your life around but feel like there are blocks stopping you. When you've tried turning it around before, you failed.

- You lack clarity around what you want in life, how to get there and what has stopped you so far.

- You want to learn how to coach yourself through challenges and towards the life you want.

- You want to discover clear strategies, tips, tools and ideas for moving forward.

- You want to feel in control, like a leader of your life.

If some or all the above resonates, well, I'm excited you're here right now, reading this and honoured to have the opportunity to serve you. I appreciate the fact you've invested the money, time and energy in me and yourself.

Let's do this!

How to use this book

Before we dive into the juicy stuff, I want to offer you one simple tip on getting the most out of the book.

Don't just *read* the insights, **live** them!

If you're anything like me, you've likely read self-help books before, or you've been given good advice, you may have even worked with a Coach/Therapist/Counsellor before. And despite gaining useful insights or advice you *know* deep down will help you, you've done nothing with them. Don't worry, there's no judgement here. I'm guilty of this too, trust me!

I've learned over the last few years, Information alone is worthless.

In the world of Personal Development, a dangerous myth that gets thrown around a lot is this...

"Information is power".

I respectfully disagree.

My truth is this...

The **right** information, when **applied** is power.

We can read all the right books, enrol in dozens of courses, work with professionals who can support us BUT unless we apply the Insights and Information, unless we take them and really live them, nothing will change.

Imagine being sat behind the wheel of a Supercar. Thanks to the engine, you've got the potential to reach speeds of more 220 MPH and with a full tank of fuel you'll be able to drive great distances. But **only** if you apply your foot on the accelerator.

To get the most out of this book, apply, apply, apply the insights from this book. Fill your tank with insights and take them for a spin. Highlight the words that resonate with you, consider the reflection questions at the end of certain chapters and complete the exercises. Your future self will thank you.

How am I qualified to write this?

This is a question my Gremlin has whispered to me time and time again. You see, I suffer occasionally with what is known as 'Imposter Syndrome'. Meaning, I sometimes have the feeling I'm a fraud.

Deep down, I know this is nonsense.

I've been in the world of Coaching since 2014 and in this time, I've developed a track record of helping people around the world to get unstuck and take charge of their lives. I've invested thousands of pounds in my own personal development through courses and Coaching. This year alone I must have read or listened to near 50 books. When it comes to understanding human behaviour, goal attainment and strategies for success, I know my stuff.

But, what makes me most qualified to write this Book, is the fact I turned my own life around 7 years ago.

You see, in my early 20s, my life looked like a mess. I'll weaving my story into the chapters, but to paint you a picture of where I was, this is what my life looked like in 2011.

- I was stuck in an unfulfilling Insurance job.

- I was hopelessly single, stuck in the 'friend zone'.

- I was overweight and unfit, living off junk-food, the only exercise I got was a walk to the kebab shop.

- I suffered with anxiety and panic attacks, often having to run into the toilet at work to throw water on my face to calm myself down.

- I was stuck in low confidence and self-esteem (which I over-compensated for by playing a Jack-the-lad role).

- I partied to numb the pain and endless stream

of fearful thoughts, partying Thursday through to Sunday, drinking enough Guinness to kill a small horse and smoking like a sailor.

- I was stuck in debt with 3 payday loan companies, struggling to make the repayments each month and keep my head above water.

The worst part was, nobody knew I was struggling.

It was all my very own dirty little secret.

To my friends and family, I was the same old happy-go-lucky, confident and happy, Will. But inside, the shame of my struggles was rotting me.

Today, I'm proud to say, my life looks very different.

This, for me, is what makes me most qualified to write this book.

The fact I was able to turn it all around and become Unstuck in many different areas of my life. I now wake up each morning and feel in control of my life.

And if I can do it, so can you.

Section One

What do I want instead?

Doom and Gloom

During my darkest days, I had a dreadful belief of *This is how it is forever*.

At the time, it made sense! I would wake up, day after day, week after week, and nothing got better. I only became more stuck; more anxious, more helpless, more broke and more miserable.

Sat at my desk at work, I'd doomily daydream, imagining myself in my 50's; still living with my parents, still working the same old office job I disliked still clinging to the thin threads of my sanity and life. Still stuck.

This thought made my blood run cold.

But this is what I focused on. In my helpless state, all I could think about all day long was not only how terrible my life was at the time but how terrible it was going to *continue* to be! Talk about a death sentence.

I didn't realise back then but through this gloomy focus, I was creating my own gloomy reality.

In life, we get more of what we focus on.

It's just the way our minds work.

When I repeatedly focus on something my mind thinks "Ok, Will is focusing on how bad his life is, it must be really important to him, let's show more of this for him".

Ta-da, more evidence to confirm my helpless story.

It wasn't that I didn't have good things in my life at the time, I was surrounded by great friends and family, and a few areas of my life were good, my social life for example! Ok, the social life was a little bit too good.

But I couldn't see this at the time because my mind would filter these areas to remain consistent with my story of "My life is all doom and gloom".

My great friend Dave had a similar experience when he was considering buying a BMW. We met up a week or so after he first thought he might buy a BMW.

"It's the weirdest thing", he said, "Since I've considered buying a BMW, it's like every car I see on the road is a BMW".

Now, it wasn't as if there were suddenly more Beamers on the road. What was happening for Dave was he was *noticing* them more.

This is the same reason, I believe, why practising gratitude can result in higher levels of happiness. It only makes sense that if one was to write down 3 things they are grateful for each day, over time they would notice even more things they're grateful for and as a result, feel a little happier.

As well as being aware that we seemingly get more of what we focus on in life, another important phenomenon to know is called the Cybernetic Loop. Put simply, our thoughts influence our feelings and our feelings influence our thoughts meaning if we're not careful we can feel stuck in a loop of negative feelings and thoughts, as the two feed of each other.

This was certainly what was happening as I Sat at my desk daydreaming.

Helpless thoughts caused me to feel helpless and because I was in a helpless state of feeling, my thoughts continued to be Helpless.

I can see clearly now, my doom and gloom

story were keeping me prisoner.

Little did I realise this core truth: **The past does not equal the future.**

Are you ready to explore your future?

Because opening the door to a different future, a different way of living is the first step towards turning things around and becoming unstuck.

It's time to explore the question, "What do I want *instead* of this?"

The 12-month Vision Exercise

The first step toward creating an improved future is developing the ability to envision it. **Vision** will ignite the fire of passion that fuels our commitment to do whatever it takes to achieve excellence. Only **vision** allows us to transform dreams of greatness into the reality of achievement through human action. **Vision** has no boundaries and knows no limits. Our **vision** is what we become in life.

— Tony Dungy

The following exercise is one I often use with my Coaching clients.

I like it because it engages the imagination and transcends us beyond our current situation. Because if we only focus on where we are now, we'll get more of it. If we focus on what we want instead, we'll begin to create it.

Make sure you complete this exercise in a place where you won't be distracted.

If possible, complete this exercise in an *inspiring* place, perhaps a beach, hotel, anywhere that's inspiring for you! Familiar environments trigger familiar thought patterns so by completing this exercise in a new inspiring environment, you'll find it easier to think new and inspiring thoughts.

If completing this exercise in an inspiring place isn't possible, and I appreciate it may not be, do your best to get into an inspired state of mind. Perhaps listen to some music you know gets you pumped up. If you're feeling stuck for a song, check out AMS by Martin Kohlstedt. I can't help but listen to this and feel inspired.

You will need something to write on, either the notes section on your phone or good old pen and paper.

I want you to begin to imagine it's exactly 12 months from today. Exactly one year since you picked up that book *Becoming Unstuck*.

Imagine you are reflecting on how life has been over the last 12 months, and it's been amazing beyond belief. It's been an amazing 12 months because everything you could wish to have happened has happened. It's almost as someone has waved a magic wand, and all your desires have been granted. You've made the changes you wanted to and you've become the person you've always dreamed of being. Life isn't just good, it's *crazy good*.

Now. Imagine you are writing a letter or

sending an email to me from 12-months in the future, sharing all the amazing things that have happened for you. Tell me what life is like now, what has changed, how *you* have changed. (You'll be writing in the past tense).

What does your professional life look like?

Your personal life? Relationships? Hobbies?

Finances? Health and fitness?

To make it feel as real as possible, engage your senses. Tell me what you see, how you feel, what you can hear and smell. Write about the types of thoughts you now have.

Remember, write as if it's *already* happened (you're 12 months into the future, remember). Whatever you write is going to be great, you can't get this wrong.

This may be tricky or it may not.

If you do find it tricky and you don't *know* what

to write, come from a place of Choice.

Steve Chandler's makes this distinction in his brilliant book *Crazy Good*.

Knowing vs Choosing.

Knowing what we want can be difficult because we feel it must be the "right choice".

I lovingly encourage you to forget knowing and start choosing. For completing this exercise and in life in general. Choice is freedom. Imagine anything is possible, as if you are choosing and placing your order with the Universe/God.

We pressure ourselves when we come from the place of knowing what the "right choice is". The truth is, only time will tell what the right choice is. Later on in the book I'll share more ideas on Decision making.

Please don't skip ahead until you've completed this exercise!

The exercise is useless unless completed so take the time to do this.

Well, how did you find it?

Did you notice just by imagining this future, you started to *feel* as if you were already there?

This is the power of the imagination.

By completing this exercise, what you have created is a Vision.

If you'd like to (and I hope you would like to, by the way) you're invited to email me your 12-month vision letter.

Firstly, because I'm proper nosey...

No, seriously, I'm curious what your vision looks like. Secondly, I will promise to resend you your vision letter exactly 12-months to the day from the day you email it to me. Sound fun? All you have to do is type it up and email it to me at will@orangeboxpd.com

Imagine 12 months from now, checking your inbox randomly to see an Email from me. You click on the Email and see your vision attached, what you'd totally forgotten about because, hey life has been crazy good, and click open. You read, the hairs on the back of your neck stand stiff as your eyes, wide with disbelief, scan the words on the screen. You realise your 12 months vision is now a reality. Wow.

Now you have created your exciting vision (and emailed it to me if you wish) I want you to reward yourself, seriously! Give yourself a pat on the back, treat yourself to a Coffee (always my reward of choice), do a happy dance - whatever you need to do to celebrate this step forward. I believe rewarding ourselves along the way is a great way to keep up momentum and encourage ourselves to keep taking steps forwards.

What you've done is taken a vital step forward. Too many people in life are Visionless, I'm pleased you are not one of them. If you wanted to, from this point onwards, you can choose to use your vision as a point of guidance.

You can ask yourself "Does the way I'm thinking/feeling/acting now take me closer towards my vision or further away"?

It's a powerful question, right? Plenty more questions like these to come.

It all starts with a Vision

As I write this book, I'm sat overlooking the crystal-clear blue sea in the beautiful country of Croatia.

I flew in yesterday from Germany and before I got down to business and began writing, I had a wander around the ancient City of Pula. One of the highlights for me was a huge stone temple. It looked like something straight out of a History Book on Ancient Rome

As I looked up at this huge creation in awe, I thought to myself *Before this existed, it was just a vision in someone's mind.*

I stood gazing for a good 10 minutes at this temple, feeling growingly smaller and more inspired as time ticked by.

Everything and I mean, everything, began life as a vision, made possible by the imagination and thoughts of a human being (or God/the Universe).

From the chair your sitting on right now to the clothes you are wearing (I assume you're wearing clothes), they all began as a vision.

A vision someone created. It started with a thought and through action was created. We'll be exploring how to create your vision in later chapters, but I really want to make this point. You, like all of us, are a powerful creator!

Reflections:

- How did it feel to imagine your 12-month vision?
- What is your greatest achievement and how did you create that?

Turning your Vision into Goals

If you set goals and go after them with all the determination you can muster, your gifts will take you places that will amaze you. - Les Brown

Now it's time to turn your vision into goals.

When I was stuck, I was goal-less which resulted in me feeling Helpless.

Nothing changed because I was doing what I had always done. Go to work. Eat. Drink beer and Party. Repeat.

Everything changed when I began to set goals for myself. For the first time in a very long time, I had a sense of direction. So rather than feeling I was swimming around in circles and treading water, I had an island to swim towards.

To create your goals, we'll be using your vision from the exercise you completed.

The magnificent 7 of Goal-Setting

To set goals successfully, there are certain criteria to bear in mind. For me, these are the 7 most important criteria to consider.

1. Specific.

When it comes to Goal-setting, the more specific the better. Vague goals are a no-no. If in your vision you wrote "Be fitter", get specific.

How fit do you want to be? How far would you like to run/swim/cycle? What does fitness look like for you exactly?

2. Measurable.

You want your goals to be measurable, so you can track your progress and success. For difficult to measure goals, like self-confidence, give a number to your current level with 10 being high, 0 being low and score yourself as of today. This way, in the future you can rescore.

3. In your control.

So much of our life isn't in our control. Other people's behaviour, the economy, the weather.

Byron Katie says there are 3 types of business in life, mine, theirs, and God's.

Make sure your goals are in your business, under your control.

4. Positive.

The mind has a tough time processing negative statements.

For example, right now DO NOT think of a ginger cat riding along on a Skateboard.

So rather than having a goal of 'I don't want to be unhealthy' where the mind can only focus on the unhealthy element, write about the health you wish to enjoy.

As a simple rule for goals, talk about what you DO want rather than what you DON'T want.

5. Written down.

Write your goals down and keep them somewhere visible, a journal, stuck on the fridge or bedroom wall, somewhere you'll be able to re-read them again and again.

Words are even more powerful when written down.

6. Timed.

A goal without a date is just a dream - Milton H. Erickson.

In the vision exercise, we went with 12-months. It may be when turning your vision statements into goals you feel 12-months is either too short or too long a time to achieve them. Attach a date for each of your goals that feels right.

7. Un-realistic.

When I started to train as a Coach, I was taught

how to set goals and was advised to make goals "Realistic".

The reason being, if you go for a goal which is unrealistic and don't achieve it, you may be disheartened.

My thoughts on this? Total rubbish.

There is nothing wrong with being disheartened, it happens! In fact, we can choose to bounce back and become even more hungry to achieve our goals when feel disheartened if we chose to.

I encourage my clients to dream big because, let's be real, who really knows what is ''realistic''? I would personally rather myself or a client fall just short on a big-ass goal than achieve a smaller, less satisfying "realistic" goal.

Norman Vincent Peale had the right Idea when he said "Shoot for the moon. Even if you miss, you'll land among the stars."

You now have clear and measurable goals to work towards, having broken down the individual elements of your Vision.

Making Goal Attainment easy

Simplicity is ultimately a matter of focus

- Ann Voskamp

I like simple. Which is why this book is short and sweet.

I want to share with you now a 'System' if you like, for making achieving your goals easy. Because you may be looking at your goals and thinking "that's all well and good, but where do I go from here"?

Later in the book, you'll learn how to Coach yourself to discover exactly what your next steps are, so for now, this is about creating a *system* for organising the steps you need to take.

What I suggest is looking at your list of goals and start by picking your top 5 goals you would like to achieve or make progress towards over the next 3 months. The 5 which, if you achieved them, would make the biggest difference in your life.

Any more than 5 goals and you may be overwhelming yourself which is how many people slip up. I used to do this. Tell myself I was going to turn everything around in my life. Come Monday (it was always going to begin on Monday), I was going to; go back to the gym, speak to so and so, start budgeting, start meditating, stop smoking and drinking etc.

And I did. For about 3 days. Then I fell back into the old and familiar way of being.

To avoid this, just 5 Goals to focus on for the next 3 months.

Got your 5 goals? Great. We'll refer to these as Long-term Goals.

At the start of each new week, you will set yourself 5 weekly goals that will relate to your 5 longer-term goals. This is called 'chunking-down'. By chunking down you'll create a nice and clear focus just for the week ahead.

For example, if one of your 5 long term goals is fitness related (to weigh a certain amount, for example), a weekly goal could be to have completed 3 gym workouts.

Again, you want no more than 5 weekly goals for the same reason, to create focus.

Next, each morning, you look at your 5 weekly goals and ask "What 3-5 steps do I need to take today in order to achieve my weekly goals"?

Continuing with the fitness example, each morning you will see one of your weekly goals is to complete 3 workouts so can decide on what days you'll make it happen and go the gym. What I like about this approach is 1. It's simple and 2. There is a real sense of focus because your daily actions directly relate to your weekly goals which relate to your longer-term goals. Simples.

If you know me, you'll know I'm a stationary geek. I'm like a teenage girl a week before they go back to School. To anyone exploring my beloved diary, you'll find it bursting with brightly coloured sticky notes. My long-term goals will be in there. My weekly goals will be stuck on the Sundays and each day has a sticky note with my top 3-5 daily steps.

Reflections:

- What are your top 5 goals for the next 3 months?
- How will you track your weekly and daily goals?

Section Two

Why am I stuck?

Next, we're going to be exploring why we stay stuck.

An important question to ask first of all is What is the benefit of being stuck?

Often when I ask this in a Coaching conversation, I'm met with confused expressions and I hear, "There is no benefit at all, Will, which is why it's so frustrating".

I respectfully disagree. Being stuck can have many benefits: approval from others, avoidance of disappointment or pain, comfort, and most of all, safety!

Because isn't it true, being stuck, although exhausting and frustrating is a safe place to be because of its familiarity?

And safety, more so, our *survival* is the number one role of the human mind.

Which means as miserable as we may be, if our minds associate more potential pain in changing than staying the same, we'll stay the same.

The key to change is to associate changing as something positive and staying the same as something negative.

Next is a great exercise for achieving this.

The Dickens Technique

This technique comes from Tim Ferris' book, *Tools of Titans* and is named the Dickens Technique because as in Charles Dickens' classic *A Christmas Carol* it explores the past, present and the future.

The purpose of this technique is to associate pain with an area you want to change, in the past, presently and in the future. Reason being, when we've associated pain with an area in the past, present and future, we can't help but feel change is needed.

First, recall a habit, behaviour you have or a situation you're in which although you know it's destructive for you, you continue to do.

It could be smoking, finally quitting the job you no longer enjoy, or a problem you've been putting off facing.

Spend a few minutes really considering each of the 3 questions below, bringing to mind examples.

So, thinking of the area you'd like to change...

Firstly, what has this negatively cost you in the past?

Physically, emotionally, financially? Bring to mind specific examples. Close your eyes and relive them, seeing what you saw, hearing what you heard and feeling what you felt.

Secondly, what is this costing your presently?

Again, consider the physical, emotional and financial costs. What are you missing out on right now because of this problem?

Lastly, what will this cost you physically, emotionally and financially in the future if nothing changes?

How will things look 5 or 10 years from now? Close your eyes and imagine a possible future scenario. Imagine how things will look, what you might hear, and importantly, how it's going to feel.

Once you've considered what your problem *has* cost you, *is* costing you, and *will* cost you, and you now feel and understand a change needs to be made, I suggest standing up and shaking off those negative feelings.

Literally, stand up and move about, shaking your arms and legs about. Doing this releases tension, it gets the issues out the tissues! I don't want you absorbing those feelings and carrying them with you for the rest of the day.

If you look at a Gazelle after it's just escaped death after being chased by a Lion, it does this. It will kick its hind legs powerfully, releasing the tension from its body. We humans aren't so good at doing this. We keep our tension stored up in our bodies.

So please, have a quick shake.

Now you've shaken off any tension, I want to invite you to think of all the positive benefits of making the change.

What will be better because of overcoming this problem once and for all? What opportunities will exist? You may like to close your eyes and imagine a future you, without this problem.

How would that feel?

How will you be better off physically, emotionally and financially?

The key with this exercise is **emotion**. You want to begin to associate more *pain* with staying the same, and *pleasure* with making the change.

If you think of a time when you've made a lasting change, leaving a toxic relationship or stopping a bad habit, you would have gone through the exact same process. You would have seen how it had caused you pain in the past, in the present and how it would cause you pain in the future too. Continuing would be too painful.

Reflections:

- Check in with yourself, how do you now feel about the area you wanted to change? Hopefully you've felt a shift, a sense of urgency for making a change once and for all. If not, you may need to repeat this exercise several times and with more intensity.

Why do you believe you haven't achieved your goals already?

This might be the most important question for you to answer in this entire book. Really. Because your answers (your words) will reveal your current reality, the way you view yourself and the world.

So truly consider this question and give it some time for your answers to arise, why do you **believe** you haven't achieved your goals already?

I recommend writing your answers out on paper, there is something powerful about taking the words out of our heads and down onto paper.

Your answers will be the blocks holding you back. The great news is, you are far more powerful than these blocks, no matter how real or scary they may seem.

In my experience, there are two main blocks stopping us from achieving our goals and getting unstuck.

Beliefs and Fears.

Beliefs

A bodybuilder from the United States was on vacation in Thailand. A lover of animals, he decided to visit the local elephant sanctuary. As a lover of strength, the American was in awe of the sheer size and potential power of the magnificent tusked beasts. There was one detail he just couldn't get his head around. The elephants weren't kept locked in big enclosures like he had seen in Zoos in the USA, no, the only thing keeping the elephants from breaking free was a rope tied around one of their legs. Stating his disbelief to one of the staff members at the sanctuary, the American said "Why is it only a single rope is holding these animals back, it's obviously not strong enough to contain an animal this strong"?

The Thai staff member smiled before answering. "You're right, if they wanted to, these big adult elephants could easily break free from the rope. But they don't know that. When they were younger and not as strong, the ropes were just enough to keep the elephants tied up. Although the elephants changed, the belief that they're too weak to break free stayed the same".

Like the elephants in the story, we all have beliefs that hold us back.

The tricky part can be discovering what these beliefs are, because often we're not aware of them. Very soon though I'll share a ridiculously easy way of becoming aware of what beliefs might be holding you back.

Briefly, though, I'll share where beliefs come from.

When we are children, we're constantly picking up beliefs. Beliefs about who we are, what we're good at, what we're not good at; beliefs about all sorts. Naturally, many of our beliefs get passed down from our parents, but we also pick up beliefs from our family, friends, teachers and society in general. In our early years, we're gathering information to make sense of the world, forming our own stories.

Many beliefs are positive, for example, as a child you may have been praised for your ability to paint. Little you will then absorb this feedback and form the belief of "I'm a good artist".

On the other hand, many beliefs we form are negative, in the world of Coaching they're referred to as *Limiting Beliefs*, because, well they limit us!

Limiting beliefs could look like:

- I'm not clever.

- I'm not important.

- I'm a bad person.

- Showing my emotions is a sign of weakness

- Money is the root of all evil

- I have to be perfect to be loved.

- I'm too old/young

Let's look at the belief of 'Showing my emotions is a sign of weakness' to see how it may be limiting.

I should mention, this belief was mine.

Culturally the world over, young boys are not encouraged to show their emotions. We hear things like "Man up" and "Big boys don't cry". Doesn't quite send the best message, right?

Growing up, I formed a story in my head that being a man and a boy is all about being strong, physically and emotionally. If you feel sad, you suck it up. This is what I did. Which was a huge issue because... I'm super sensitive!

I definitely inherited my sensitivity from my mum, because, bless her cotton socks, she's super sensitive too.

Saturday evenings as a child, my brother, sister, parents and I would sit around the television and watch Saturday night TV together. Typically, we'd watch Pop Idol, which if you don't know, was a talent show where aspiring singers would compete to win a contract with a music label.

As you can imagine, emotions ran high in this contest.

Contestants dreams were shattered each week and as the weeks went by and as the grand final grew nearer it got more emotional. During the final few stages, when a contestant was eliminated, they would play a montage of the singer's journey, showing snippets of video footage from the first audition and their journey up until the moment of elimination.

In the bottom right-hand corner of the television screen would be the singer's live reaction of their highlight reel and, of course, they were sobbing their eyes out.

My dear mum would be sat on the Sofa opposite me, sobbing uncontrollably too, a box of tissues on her lap which she always had "just in case".

I remember each week, sitting there with the biggest lump in my throat, as Coldplay's "Fix you" would play over the singer's montage of memories. I desperately wanted to cry. But I can't remember ever crying. Not once. Ever.

I sat there, putting on a brave face. Keeping my emotions bottled up.

My parents are great, and I know now full well I could have cried openly in front of them, but I didn't. Because at some point early in life, I don't know when or where exactly, I picked up this belief that Men showing their emotions is a sign of weakness.

This belief became more limiting as I grew older and I know it was a huge contributing factor to my living with anxiety in my early 20s.

I suffered in silence for far too long.

Ignoring my emotions and not expressing how I really felt.

Eventually, it got to the point where I couldn't contain my emotions any longer.

After having a huge panic attack one dark Sunday night, it was time to talk. So on the Monday morning, accompanied by my Dad, I visited the Doctors. I told my Doc how I felt, sharing my struggles and emotions.

I felt as if a weight had been lifted from my shoulders, not a huge weight, but a significant one. Although I didn't realise it, I was forming a new belief around showing my emotions. I was creating a new story.

Original Belief: Showing my emotions is a sign of weakness

New Belief: Showing my emotions is healthy and normal.

Living out this new belief, I felt free. I opened up to my parents about my struggles and their toll on my emotions. I shared with my close friends and colleagues what I was going through. And with each conversation, I strengthened this new belief. People were totally understanding and accepting of me, which helped to confirm it really was Ok to show my emotions.

Re-writing your Limiting Beliefs in 4 Steps

Here are 4 steps you can take to re-write your Limiting Beliefs.

1. Identify your Limiting Beliefs.

A simple way of doing this is to go back and look at your goals and consider what you're 'Yeah buts' are.

For example: I want to be fit and healthy, YEAH BUT I'm a lazy person.

Limiting belief: I'm Lazy.

I want a promotion at work YEAH BUT I'm not manager material.

Limiting Belief: I don't have what it takes to take on a Managerial role.

I want to start a new career YEAH BUT I'm too old.

Limiting Belief: I'm too old to start a new Career.

2. What evidence do I have for and against the Belief?

This is a really important step.

Rarely, we stop to challenge our limiting beliefs and see how true they are in the present moment.

For your limiting beliefs, ask what recent, solid, evidence do I have to show it's true?

3. Rewrite your Limiting Beliefs so they feel free, allow growth, and empower you!

Limiting belief: I'm Lazy.

New Belief: I'm motivated in the areas of my life that are in important to me.

Limiting belief: I don't have what it takes to take on a Managerial role.

New Belief: Every day, I can develop the skills I need in order to be a Manager.

Limiting belief: I'm too old to start a new Career.

New Belief: My life Experience will help me in starting a new Career.

If your limiting beliefs are about your ability (for example, I'm a terrible public speaker) you can rewrite with the sentence starter

"Everyday, in every way, I'm getting better and better at... (public speaking).

4. Continue to gather evidence for your New Beliefs.

Ask yourself, how can I behave in a way that is consistent with this new belief?

If I truly believed this, what would I do?

Remember: You are free to decide your decisions and actions. You have what it takes to behave in a new way that is consistent with your new beliefs.

Beliefs are the mind-made boundaries of possibility. With new beliefs, come new possibilities! Are you excited?

There must be something wrong with me

"Es tut mir leid, ich spreche kein Deutsch".

For those of you who don't speak German, this means "I'm sorry, I don't speak German".

Which I've always found hilarious - when someone says they cannot speak the language they are speaking in.

Anyways, when I first moved to Germany in 2015, I was saying a lot of this.

And it was keeping me stuck.

Before moving when I was in the UK I had

learned the basics, how to introduce myself, talk about the weather, order a beer, you know, the essential stuff.

But I soon learned whilst out and about in the City centre among the locals, this wasn't going to get me very far.

The moment I was spoken to and I didn't understand 100%, I would freeze, like a helpless rabbit in the headlights and mutter "Es tut mir leid, ich spreche kein Deutsch".

A few months passed and I was beginning to feel frustrated because I'd barely learned any new words since moving.

I soon realised why.

Every time I had frozen and said I didn't speak German, I was unknowingly creating the story that "I'm just not good at learning languages".

This limiting belief was holding me back and it was a deep one because it wasn't a limiting belief about languages being difficult to learn, no, it was personal! It was about ME.

How **I** was just no good at learning languages.

This, in my eyes, is the most restricting type of limiting belief, when it's personal. I hear this a lot with my clients, they too convince themselves the reason they are stuck is because of some defect in their personality.

They were just not born with the "language learning gene" or the "self-discipline gene".

It simply isn't true.

Because it's not a personality thing, it's a pattern thing.

Let me show you.

Here was my 'perfect pattern' for creating the

belief "I'm just not good at learning languages":

- The second someone speaks to me in German and I don't understand everything perfectly, freeze and say "Es tut mir leid, I spreche kein Deutsche".

- Stay in my comfort zone, saying only the words I know.

- Make no effort what so ever to learn more of the German language.

- Only speak in English with Yvonne at home (she is native German).

- Only speak English with other German friends.

The pattern worked perfectly... in confirming my story.

Luckily, I was able to spot how I was creating this pattern. This wasn't a personality thing at all, in fact, it turns out I'm pretty good at languages BUT only when I allow myself to learn. (More about the principle of Permission later on).

I had to ask myself, *what do I want instead of this?*

Simple, I wanted to speak a level of German where I could at least get by.

I got to work at designing a new pattern...

First of all, I'd need to stop shooting myself in the foot when interacting with the locals. I decided to instead reply with "Es tut mir leid, ich komme aus England und lerne Deutsche, noch mal bitte'. Which translates to "I'm sorry, I come from England and am learning German, can you repeat what you said again please".

Before I knew it, I was engaging in conversations and picking up new words and phrases thick and fast. This new way of responding was just what I needed.

My new pattern looked like this:

- Saying "I'm sorry I come from England and am learning German, can you repeat what you said please", instead.

 - Getting out of my comfort zone and starting to use the new words I was picking up during a conversation.

 - Making an effort in learning German, learning new words and phrases per day.

 - Insisting on speaking more German with German friends instead of English.

- Working with a private tutor.

The new pattern worked. Now I speak a decent level of German, I'm not fluent but I speak at a level where I can get by.

When you want a different result, create a new pattern.

Don't believe the problem is down to your personality. It's not, it's only ever a Pattern.

Will Aylward

Exercise: Creating a new Pattern

1. Bring to mind an ongoing struggle.

2. What is the current pattern and how do you create it?

Bullet point the elements that make up this pattern, the decisions and actions.

3. What do you want instead?

4. What would an improved pattern look like based on what you would like instead?

Bullet point the new elements to create the new pattern.

What Fear might be Stopping you?

Expose yourself to your deepest fear; after that, fear has no power, and the fear of freedom shrinks and vanishes. You are free.

— Jim Morrison

Fear and limiting beliefs are two sides of the same coin.

With my 'I'm just not good at languages' belief, the fear was of failing and looking stupid.

They fuel each other and to move forward both Limiting Beliefs and Fears need to be conquered. So consider this question for a moment, what Fear might be stopping you from moving you forward?

This may be difficult because (like limiting beliefs) fears are often sneaky little things, lingering beneath the surface avoiding capture.

Once you capture your Fear, write it down on paper. Like I said in a previous chapter, there is something powerful about writing words down on paper.

Get your Fears written down.

In my opinion, based on the hundreds of conversations I've had with my coaching clients, there are two Fears I hear time and time again.

1. The Fear of Failure.

2. The Fear of Disapproval.

I want to offer some ideas on both of these fears because as Franklin D Roosevelt said in his inaugural address "There is nothing to Fear except Fear itself".

Fear of Failure

I developed a Fear of Failure when I was 13 years old.

It was the end of Year 8 and I received some news that made my heart sink into my stomach. In Year 9 I would be moving down one class for *all* subjects.

The news hit me hard. This move down meant being split apart from my best mate, Alex, which was super tragic for me because we'd been in the same classes since reception. Being moved down, in my eyes, meant I had failed.

I'd always worked hard in school and up until this point in my life, I was getting good grades. This year, however, I'd failed Science and my teacher, Mr Moller, had suggested I moved down a class. I was furious! My blood boiled when I spotted Mr Moller walking around the school.

This was my first real taste of Failure, and it was bitter.

Unbeknownst to me, this experience would have an impact on me for years to come.

Subconsciously, 13-year-old me, created a 'Perfect Pattern' for avoiding any future pain from failure.

The pattern was this: **give about 70% effort in everything I did.**

From this point, up until I became aware of the pattern through working with a Coach at the age of 23, I never gave it my all. Every academic test, every job, every relationship, I always gave less than my best.

In this 70% effort pattern, I couldn't lose, the pattern was bloody genius!

Because if through giving 70% I still succeeded in my eyes, e.g. I passed a test, then great, I'd pat myself on the back.

Even when I did fail, it didn't hurt because I could always comfort myself by saying *well you didn't succeed but you didn't give 100% so it's not a true reflection so it doesn't matter*.

Clever, right?

Sure, the pattern worked perfectly in protecting me from the pain of failure, but my 70% approach robbed me of a deep sense of fulfilment.

I would wonder... *What if?*

What if I gave 100%? What would have happened? How well could I have done?

I share the story of my 70% pattern with clients who have a Fear of Failure too and it's met with nodding heads and an "Aha" as they realise they are running on a similar pattern.

If you're recognising a Fear of Failure in your

own life, here are 3 approaches for living with your FOF.

1. Failure is a judgement from you, not a definition of you.

I love to watch documentaries, especially documentaries set in American prisons. I'll never forget one particular episode. The crew were interviewing a man in his 50's who had been in and out of prison his whole life.

"My whole life I was told I was a failure, that I'd never amount to anything in life. My life was in the streets. I made bad, bad decisions which got me here. I guess they were right".

My heart broke listening to this guy, who was clearly smart with heaps of potential he could tap into. But his story had always been he'd turn out to be a failure.

I wish I could have gone back in time and met this guy before he took to the streets and began living a life of crime. I would Coach him around his mindset, help him to tap into his potential. Most of all, I would help him to see he is not a failure.

Because I don't believe anyone can ever *be* a Failure.

In the same way, someone cannot ever *be* a Success.

Neither identities are possible because they are nothing more than judgements, Success and Failure look different for everyone.

Failure is a judgement, it's not an identity.

Realising this is important because judgements can be changed.

If I were to ask you to consider one of your famous failures in life, I guarantee I could help you to see it wasn't a total failure. Because hidden within this "Failure" would be lessons, insights, developed strengths and positive elements.

Anytime you have a setback in life, rather than letting the mind label it as a total failure. Consider the following questions.

- What positive benefit has this had on my life?

- What can I learn about myself?

- What can I learn in general?

2. I never lose

I never lose. I either win or learn. - Nelson Mandela.

Imagine living life from this place.

Feeling failure or losing is impossible.

If you're willing to search for the lessons - it's possible.

The greatest people in history have all had a similar approach to Failure, perhaps this is one of the biggest factors separating the Ordinary from the Extraordinary?

As Thomas Edison said "I have not failed. I've just found 10,000 ways that won't work.

Because failure is nothing more than a judgement, it means we get to choose for ourselves what a failure looks like. We needn't confirm to someone else's idea of what a failure is.

3. Toddler vs Teenager approach to fear of failure.

In hindsight, 13-year-old me was really hard on himself for getting moved down a class. But as teenagers, we're generally unforgiving of ourselves. Running high on hormones and feeling the pressures of growing up, we start to lose the easy-going attitude we once had as children.

I'm all for the **toddler's approach to failure**.

If a toddler falls when learning to walk, they don't stay down, give up, beat themselves up or believe this makes them a failure.

No, a toddler laughs it off as their parent says "Whoops-a-daisy".

And even if it's slowly, they do their best to pull themselves up to standing and they try again to walk. They'll fall and get back up over and over again, until one day, they've cracked it.

Reflections:

- What personal "failures" can you turn around and view in a different light?
- How can you be more Toddler and less Teenager when it comes to failure?

Fear of Disapproval

It's better to be hated for what you are than to be loved for what you are not

- Andre Gide.

The second big fear I see time and time again is the Fear of Disapproval.

I've spoken with business owners who struggle to make sales because of a fear of being too pushy. I've had calls with people who've never acted on their dreams because they fear what their family/friends/neighbours, would think of them.

Although this fear can be frustrating, it has a worthy intention.

Our distant ancestors lived in far smaller communities compared to today. They realised that surviving on their own was a real struggle, so it made sense to live in small tribes to share the responsibilities and watch out for one another. That way, if one hunter failed to catch dinner, it was Ok because a fellow hunter in the community would share his catch. It only makes sense to comply and contribute, not rock the boat and upset people. To do so would mean banishment from the community which made chances of survival far harder.

I think we have this same fear ingrained in us today.

Ever say Yes to someone when you'd rather say no? I know I have.

If you believe you may have a Fear of Disapproval, here are 3 big ideas I hope will help.

1. Don't regret not being yourself

In the book titled *the top 5 regrets of the Dying* the most common regret of all was...

I wish I'd had the courage to live a life true to myself, not the life others expected of me.

Imagine how tragic it must feel to get the end of your life only to realise you've spent your entire time here on Earth, not being true to yourself. Presenting an inauthentic version of who you really are. That's got to hurt. I don't want to discover how that's got to feel and I don't want you to either.

Who is the *real* you? Only you can answer this.

An idol of mine, Deepak Chopra makes this powerful distinction between Self Image (what other people think of us) and Self-Referral (who we really are) in his book *The Ultimate Happiness Prescription*.

"One side of the coin is we crave approval because it bolsters our self-image, the other side is we fear disapproval because it diminishes our self-image. All of this is known as object referral which means that you identify with objects outside yourself (people, events and situations, physical objects).

The opposite of object referral is self-referral, which means you identify with your true being, entirely an inner experience. True being has 5 qualities. None of which is created by external things, events, or other people.

1. True being is connected to all that exists.

2. It has no limitations.

3. It has infinite creativity.

4. It is fearless and willing to step into the

unknown.

5. Intention from the level of being is powerful and can orchestrate synchronicity, a perfect meshing of outside circumstances to bring about your intention.

Shifting your sense of identity to your true being frees you to create a life of abundance, joy and fulfilment. Being tied to external things (the opinions of others) leaves you stranded on a superficial level of existence".

When I read this for the first time, I felt excited because the words spoke such truth.

The 5 qualities do describe our true nature because we're far more than our current life situation and far more than the opinions of others.

Life is short, and we get to choose what we focus on.

We can focus on what other people might think of us (which isn't in our control).

Or we can focus on who we really are, our unlimited potential, and living a life true to ourselves. If we don't, we might live to regret it.

Reflections:

- The REAL me is... what is true for you?
- One way I will start to live my life truer to myself is by...

2. Don't take it personally

How people treat other people is a direct reflection of how they feel about themselves.

- Paulo Coelho

I've learned not to take things personally. I used to really take it to heart if I received a negative comment on a YouTube video or a Facebook post. I'll be honest, writing this book has caused fear-of-disapproval-esque thoughts to pop up.

Images of 1 Star Amazon reviews with derogatory words saying how reading this book was an utter waste of time. Emails from people who've taken time out of their day to tell me what a terrible writer I am.

Hey, this might happen! But it's Ok if it does. The world will keep on spinning and there will be people who get value from this book. I'm not expecting EVERYONE to love this Book. I'm certainly not everyone's cup of tea, neither is my writing style, the stories I'm sharing or ideas.

The same goes for you.

Not everyone is going to approve of you and how you choose to live your life.

Meaning we have a choice, my friend. We can choose to take other people's opinions of who we are and what we do *personally*, or we can realise how other people treat us is a reflection of themselves.

We needn't take it personally.

3. Start approving of yourself

What do you mean I have to wait for someone's approval? I'm someone. I approve. So I give myself permission to move forward with my full support.

— Richelle E. Goodrich

Imagine for a moment you completely approved of yourself.

As we say in England "Warts and all".

How would that look for you?

How would it feel... to completely approve of yourself?

Truth is, it's more normal for people to criticise themselves than approve of themselves. The fear is, if we were to live a life approving of ourselves, someone may interpret this as arrogance or narcissism and then disapprove.

However, if we were to truly approve of ourselves, it simply wouldn't matter whether we are approved of or not.

Because we'd feel whole already.

True approval of ourselves isn't arrogance.

I'm sure you can think of people who totally approve of themselves and who are a world away from being arrogant? They radiate confidence. They know they're not perfect, yet they accept and approve of themselves regardless.

A powerful way to start walking the path to approving of ourselves comes from the late Louise Hay. She suggested repeating the affirmation "I approve of myself" throughout the day. Anytime you have a spare moment to think, say to yourself internally "I approve of myself". I experimented with this for a while and the result was life-changing.

I should say, I used to think affirmations were

pointless. I was a big affirmation sceptic. How could saying statements to yourself be effective, especially if they went against what I believed to be true?

I was missing the point of what affirmations were. Every thought we experience, every sentence we say is an affirmation.

When we tell ourselves, we are terrible and useless: it's an affirmation.

When we dwell on how stuck we are, it's an affirmation.

And the affirmations we continually affirm become our truths.

At first, there was resistance when I experienced the thought "I approve of myself".

It just didn't feel right. Since our feelings and thoughts are entwined, I connected with the thoughts following my affirmation to shed some light on what caused the feeling of resistance. Sure enough... It was my Gremlin. Commentating "Yeah, right".

Regardless, I persisted and very soon, it started to feel **good** to say "I approve of myself". It felt good to drop the judgements I held about myself; my beer belly, my crooked teeth. It felt like returning home.

Pause for a moment, close your eyes and tell yourself you approve of yourself.

If like me, there's resistance, begin by saying "I am willing to approve of myself". This is a great first step if there's too much resistance to the affirmation. For the next 7 days, tell yourself you approve of yourself. Anytime you have a spare second, choose to think "I approve of myself".

Section Three

Moving Forward

If you always do what you've always done,
you'll always get what you've always got

— Henry Ford

By now you've gained clarity on what you want and what might be holding you back.

Remember, what you focus on you'll get more of in your life.

Although it's always good to understand what might be holding us back, we don't want to be focusing all our time and energy on this which can lead to analysis paralysis!

Instead, we want to focus on what we **do** want and possible *solutions* for becoming unstuck.

In this part of the book, you'll learn how to tap into the power of your intuition.

To begin, I want to show you an exercise called 20 Ways.

Exercise: 20 Ways

I moved to Germany from England in April 2015.

It was a huge jump for me because as I wrote earlier, my German was minimal. On top of this, I had no job lined up, all I had was my boundless optimism and a newly formed business with a handful of paying clients. Not quite the solid foundation one would like to start a life abroad.

But I like taking risks and believe greatness happens when you dive into the deep end when you have no choice but to make a plan work out!

I'd been living in Germany for a few months and although I was loving life in the country and my heart was content now that I was living with Yvonne (after a year and a half doing the whole long-distance dating thing), my business wasn't where I wanted it to be. I wanted more clients!

I decided to work with a Coach again to help me move forward.

In between calls, I'd be given homework and one of my homework tasks was to come up with 20 ways I could create new coaching clients.

Truthfully, my first reaction was *jeez, 20 ways, sounds like a lot*.

Nevertheless, I put aside some time to complete the task.

I was amazed at how effective the exercise was. In the beginning, it was slow going, but soon the cogs in my mind were spinning faster and faster. So fast mind was too fast for me to capture all the ideas on paper.

Within no time at all, my homework task was complete. In front of me, written down on paper, I had 20 solid ideas I could follow through with to create my new coaching client.

How to play 20 ways:

1. Think of a specific current challenge, struggle or problem you are faced with. Write it down on paper.

2. Write out "20 ways to" and then state what you want *instead* of the problem down on paper, state the result you want.

For example, 20 ways to create coaching clients. 20 ways to save my relationship or 20 ways to find a new job.

3. Start writing and don't stop until you've come up with 20 possible ways to get what you want.

20 ways works because it shifts your focus from the problem to the solution. You know more than you think you know.

I really believe this.

In my Coaching practice, time and time again, I help people discover the answers for themselves. Sure, I offer insight and tools, but I can always rely on my clients to find the answers within themselves if they go looking for them.

The biggest myth around coaching and Coaches is we are these guru-like figures who has all the answers and openly shares their infinite wisdom with their clients.

I'm not a guru and luckily, to be a great Coach I don't have to be.

I know my best tool I have is... Questions.

At the end of the day, the questions we ask of ourselves determine the type of people that we will become

— Leo Babauta

Below I will share some of my favourite Coaching questions, ones I'll typically ask when a client and I are coming up for solutions to problems or discussing how to move forward to achieve goals.

So, let's play.

Let's imagine we're in a Coaching conversation, you've shared with me your inspiring vision. We've set some goals and have explored what might be holding you back.

Now it's time to brainstorm options for your next steps. I'm going to ask you some questions and you're going to share whatever comes up for you.

I know I keep banging on about this, but please write your answers down!

When answering the questions, you could consider your vision in general or you can think about each individual goal you've set for yourself. You can even return to these questions to come up with your daily steps.

You ready? Ok, let's go.

Who do you need to become?

Thinking of your inspiring vision for the future, who do you need to become?

Too often when we set ourselves goals in life, we dive into the *doing mode* by thinking about what we must *do* to achieve our goals. First, consider who you need to *be*.

The person who got you here, won't get you there.

You're going to need to tap into different strengths and characteristics that exist inside of you.

Think of your vision. What 5 adjectives best describe who you need to become to make your vision a reality?

I recommend writing these words on sticky notes and dotted them around your house to remind you how you need to be showing up in the world.

What is your next best move?

By asking yourself *what is my next best move*, you'll be strengthening your intuition, the internal guidance system we all have.

Have you ever ignored your gut-feeling only to regret it?

I know I have. There's also been plenty of times I've listened to the gut-feeling and it's worked out. I may not have got the result I was looking for straight away, but I've learned an important lesson or gained a deep insight into something. Remember, I either win or I learn!

Who can help?

No one can do the important work except ourselves, but we can absolutely ask for help along the way. In fact, it may be near to impossible to get unstuck and move forward in some cases without asking for help.

One morning during my stuck days, I was close to breaking point with my personal debt. After months of ignoring my money issues, I finally sat down and took stock of just how bad it was.

That day, I made a decision which changed everything...

I asked for help with my money problems.

I discovered an online debt help agency.

There was a form I could fill out to request a call back from one of the debt advisors.

My hands were trembling as I typed my financial struggles in the form. This was the first time I'd 'gotten real' with myself. Up until this point, I was massively in denial about the extent of my pay-day loan debts.

I submitted the form and went downstairs to make myself a cup of coffee.

It must have been about 5 minutes since I submitted the form and my mobile was buzzing in my pocket.

I answered. It was a lady from the debt agency. She had a soothing voice. I don't remember her name but I wish I did because I would like to thank her.

She asked questions. I spoke. She listened. I don't recall exactly what we spoke about, but what I'll always remember was how, as I hung up, a huge weight was lifted from my shoulders and chest.

In a few minutes, we'd created a debt plan I could present to the companies I'd owed money to. It was so easy. In my head, I'd created a story and in doing so I'd convinced myself getting help would be difficult and expensive. Plus, I imagined I'd be super ashamed to get real with someone about my debts.

My experience was the complete opposite. Getting help was easy. It was free (this debt help provider was a UK charity). And rather than feeling ashamed, I felt understood. The lady didn't judge me in the slightest, she spoke softly and with compassion.

Whatever stories you may tell yourself about asking for help, drop them.

Asking for help doesn't make us weak.

As Rona Barrett said "The strong individual is the one who asks for help when he needs it."

What is a scary step forward?

Moving forward can be scary.

Where we are, is familiar, even if it's not what we want.

But what if the way forward was scary for a reason?

What if the way forward was scary because it was there to teach you - you are more powerful than your fears?

What steps are you fearful about taking? Is it asking for help? Is it making the decision you've been putting off making for a while?

I watched a great video recently, in which Will Smith tells a story about sky diving. Type in

'Will Smith - Sky Dive' online to watch it. He shines a light on the funny nature of fear, it's strongest BEFORE we do the scary thing. He was most fearful, in the plane and the whole night *before* he skydived. The moment he should have been most fearful, when he was flying through the air at 120 mph, he wasn't fearful.

If you couldn't fail, what would you do?

A great question to come back to.

Why? It can be tempting to play it safe, to only take actions we feel comfortable taking (which are normally actions we've taken before). We've got to be willing to get uncomfortable. We've got to be willing to fail. Remember, failure is only ever a judgement from us, not a definition of us. By asking this question, we access answers we perhaps wouldn't consider.

I once Coaching a woman at a Career crossroads and she was feeling stuck.

She had several job options and didn't know what to do.

I asked her ''If you couldn't fail, what would you do''?

''That's an interesting question'', she replied, chuckling.

She knew exactly what she would do if she knew she couldn't fail.

The real issue was her self-confidence, not that she didn't know what to do.

What would your best-self do?

I don't conform to the idea of a fixed self or a fixed personality.

Because there are moments we are all lazy and there are moments we are all motivated, so to label ourselves as "lazy" is only true some of the time. More so, we can choose to develop certain attributes, we can choose to behave the way we want.

Tony Robbins has this to say to people who say they're unmotivated.

"If I put a gun to your head and told you I would pull the trigger unless you took those actions you've been putting off, would you find a way to be motivated"?

Now, we don't have to have a gun put to our heads to inspire our best behaviour. Instead, we can ask the question "What would my best self-do in this scenario"?

Because, although I don't believe in the idea of a fixed personality, I do believe we all have a "best self". The best self who handles situations the right way. The best self who follows through with actions after committing. The best self who chooses to listen to intuition and gut feelings and doesn't ignore it.

What has worked for you already?

It's helpful to look back at times in the past when we've been stuck before, to look for what has worked already in becoming unstuck.

Even if your situation is different now, there may be transferable knowledge or skills you can apply today.

What strengths do you have to help you move forward?

I find it sad how most people can easily reel off their weaknesses or what is 'wrong' with them yet find it difficult or embarrassing to talk about their strengths.

Consider what your strengths are and as you do, notice a feeling of confidence growing.

What would your role model tell you to do?

I love this question.

When my clients are stuck at coming up with solutions based on what they personally could do to move forward, I'll ask this question to change perspective.

I'll ask them to imagine sitting down with their role model, whether this is a celebrity, a parent or a friend, and ask them what advice, what gems of wisdom they would hear.

It works like a treat. Sometimes just a little change of perspective is all it takes for the answers to come through.

Alternatively, I may ask:

If this situation wasn't your own but your best friend's, what would you tell them to do?

This question also works like a treat.

Reflections:

- What was your favourite question and what resonated with you?
- What other questions could you ask yourself?

Section Four

Making it happen

Welcome to section 4.

We're going to start with a Quick Quiz.

There are 7 Frogs sat on a Log.

3 Frogs decide to jump. How many Frogs are left on the Log?

The answer is 7. *Deciding* to jump and *actually* jumping are two different things.

Are you ready to jump?

If so, you'll want to keep reading because in this part of the book I'm sharing how to take your vision, goals, actions and MAKE IT HAPPEN. These are the exact tools and Ideas my clients and I use to stay on track.

Get off of Auto-pilot

It's estimated we experience around 10,000 thoughts per day.

Most of these thoughts are the same thoughts we experienced yesterday and the majority, I'm sure you've noticed are negative.

I've always compared this habitual way of thinking to being on auto-pilot. If we make no conscious effort to thinking differently, then we fall victim to the repetitive and negative thoughts from yesterday.

We want to avoid auto-pilot-mode because our thoughts determine the choices we make. Our choices create our actions and behaviours. Our actions determine our experiences and it's our experiences that create our feelings.

To get off auto-pilot, we must create new streams of thoughts and the best time to do this is first thing in the morning, because as the old saying goes "Win the morning and you'll win the day."

A simple way of getting off auto-pilot is to spend 5 minutes first thing each morning reading over your vision and goals, including your goals for the day. By doing this, you're setting a clear intention of what success looks like in the long-term and short-term. Which is far more effective than merely drifting throughout your day without any direction. When we drift, we go into auto-pilot mode where our habitual thoughts are running the show.

If you're more visual, you may prefer to create a vision board (visit www.willaylward.com to get a free guide on how to create one). Vision boards are a visual representation of your vision and goals. It's important to have your vision board somewhere visible where you'll pass it several times throughout the day, for example on the fridge or on your desk.

Another way to get off auto-pilot is to set up silent alarms on your phone to go off at various points through the day, with a question or words that will act as a trigger and remind you of your intentions.

Affirmations are also a good option.

Reflections:

- How will you get off of Auto-pilot and remind yourself of your new way of thinking and behaving?

Schedule, Schedule, Schedule

Once you're clear on WHAT actions you'll be taking, get clear on exactly WHEN you'll be taking them. The mind loves clarity so give it clarity by writing down *what* actions you'll be taking and *when*. The act of writing something down shows it is important.

Think back to when someone attractive has given you their telephone number.

Chances are (unless you've got a memory like Rain man) you didn't just take a 'mental note'. No, you wrote the number down on the back of your hand, on a receipt, or store it in your phone. You took a written-down note of some form, because getting the hottie's number was IMPORTANT to you.

Your action steps are important to you. Without them, nothing changes.

Create the habit of getting clear on *when* you're taking steps forwards and write them down in your diary or on your phone. Take pride in being someone who follows through with their commitments, tell yourself "I am someone who sticks to their commitments, when I schedule something, it gets done"!

Reflections:

- How will you choose to stay organised and schedule?

Do it your way

To think I did all that

And may I say - not in a shy way

Oh no, oh no, not me,

I did it my way

- Frank Sinatra.

I cannot guarantee the tools and ideas in this book will work for you exactly as I prescribe them.

Sure, I'm confident they are valuable for lots of people but at the end of the day, what's worked for someone else may not work for you. Remember to do things YOUR WAY. This may look like taking on board an idea from this book, but tweaking it, making it your own, so it serves you best.

I was recently coaching a client who hired me to help her with her mindset on losing weight. She was feeling frustrated with herself because she hadn't been sticking to the workout plan she set for herself, even though the month before she had lost 10 pounds on this plan.

"What's stopped you from sticking to the plan?" I asked her gently.

She was silent as she gave my question some thought.

"It's the warm-up!", she exclaimed, "It's so long, it takes more time than the actual work out itself and I don't like most of the stretches."

I reminded her, *she* was the one who gets to choose. *She* makes the rules. *She* is the boss.

Just because someone had suggested a certain warm-up for the workout, doesn't mean she has to follow it to the T. She was no longer in school.

"How can you make this your own?", I asked curiously.

The excitement grew in her voice as she shared with me how she was going to be doing the stretches SHE enjoys in a warm-up, ones that work for her.

"Now when you think about the workout, what's the feeling"?

"It just feels good", she replied.

No matter whether your goals are fitness related, to do with building your dream business, public speaking or even chicken farming, how can you do it YOUR way?

Reflections:

- How can you make your action steps your own, so it feels natural and enjoyable?

Get Accountability

When we seek accountability, we're more
inclined to make our ability count.

- Will Aylward.

In the late 1920's some fascinating experiments
started in a factory in Chicago, USA.

Workers were split into two groups to see the
difference physical conditions had on the
worker's productivity. For one group of
workers, physical conditions stayed the same
(the control group). For the other group, the
lights in their work area became brighter.

Interestingly, the workers in the second group
showed increased productivity. More
interesting still, even when the second group's
lights were dimmed back to normal, they were
still more productive. What was causing this? It
wasn't the lights.

The phenomenon is known as the observer effect (and the Hawthorne effect, after the name of the suburb in Chicago where the factory was). The observer effect suggests the worker's productivity increased not because of the physical conditions (better lighting) but because they were being observed! Someone was showing an interest and **tracking** in their performance.

How can you increase your productivity through accountability?

Share your intentions with other people.

There's a very good reason why I've set myself a clear deadline for finishing writing this book and shared this date with several people. Left to my own devices, it's easy for me to extend the deadline... procrastinate... take a long nap... sing Karaoke alone on You Tube (I really do this sometimes). In the back of my mind, if I don't finish the first draft of this book by the date I set, I'm going to receive some messages. A bit of positive pressure can work wonders.

In my eyes, the best person to hold you accountable is a Coach or Mentor.

They want what is best for you, which may involve some tough love.

Joining a community of people on the same path as you, online or in the real world, is another great way of being held accountable. This may be why groups such as Weightwatchers have a good success rate, they have a strong sense of community and with community comes accountability.

Of course, we can also rely on friends and family to hold us accountable.

My best friend used to email his Dad at the start of each morning with his intentions for that day and his old man would check in with him in the evening.

Reflections:

- Who do I know who can hold me accountable to my intentions and personal standard?

Start Small and get Disciplined

You won't find me writing much about motivation.

Don't get me wrong, I love a motivating YouTube video as much as the next Self-development nut. But, honestly, I find Motivation over-rated and not something worth fixating on.

Why? Because of its fleeting nature. It comes and it goes.

Some mornings we wake up and want to take on the world, others we can barely pull ourselves out of bed. It's impossible to feel 100% motivated, 100% of the time.

People seem shocked when I tell them I'm not always motivated.

Their eyes look at me in surprise and I can almost see the words etched in their pupils "but you're a Life Coach, don't you have to be motivated constantly"? Makes me chuckle. No, my friend.

Instead of motivation, what I focus on building is **discipline.**

Because if you think about it, what we really need in moments when we don't want to put in the work is **discipline**. Regardless of whether we feel motivated or feel like it, we can act, all it requires is discipline.

I've been using this handy little tool consistently over the last few years and it's saved me in moments when motivation was low. It's helped me do my tax returns, put pen to paper, and - more times than I can care to remember - do the dishes.

What I do is grab an egg timer (you can use an alarm on your phone if you don't own an egg timer) and set it to 5 minutes.

I tell myself "Right, Will, old boy. For the next 5 minutes, you are doing the washing up."

I'll then proceed to wash up for 5 minutes. I'll always stick some music on too.

After 5 minutes, the egg timer sounds.

I have never stopped washing up after the 5 minutes are up.

My hands are wet, I've started to make progress with the pile of dirty dishes and I'm feeling pretty good about myself for getting started.

It's getting started which is the hardest part!

Think about it. If you feel unmotivated to go to the Gym, it's highly unlikely once you've set foot in the Gym you'll turn around and head home. You've been disciplined enough to get there, you're going to follow through.

If your motivation is at a low, start small and focus on developing discipline. Commit to just 5 minutes of action and if you carry on (it's likely you will) then great, but if not, celebrate the 5 minutes you've done. Take the smallest step forward you can.

Progress over perfection, always.

Reflections:

- How else can you build self-discipline?

Get Obsessed

The secret of change is to focus all your energy not on fighting the old, but on building the new.

- Dan Millman

Obsession is a dirty word.

We've been told it's not good to be obsessed, it's not healthy.

Be focused, but not too focused, otherwise you'll become obsessed.

Think of anyone who has achieved the extraordinary and in the eyes of the masses, they would have seemed obsessed.

What if obsession could be a good thing after all?

I think it all depends on what we're obsessing over.

If we're obsessing over how useless we are, how much our life sucks, how the past was terrible and how the future looks even bleaker, then yes, not a great idea.

But what if we were to become obsessed with our vision for the future?

Were obsessed with learning what we need to learn to take charge of our lives?

Were obsessed with becoming the person we've always dreamed of being.

Well. That would feel very different, wouldn't it?

Looking back at my early 20s when I was stuck, I can see now how obsession really served me. In the midst of the darkness, I decided I needed to take some drastic steps in order to take charge of my life.

What I needed most was to learn the value of money, face my anxiety, re-connect with my confidence, and learn to love myself.

Spontaneously one evening after work, I applied for a working-holiday visa in New

Zealand.

A few days later, my visa was granted, and I put a deposit down on a one-way flight to Auckland. From the moment I booked the flight, I became *obsessed* about my trip.

At work, I daydreamed non-stop about climbing mountains, swimming in the sea, working on farms, meeting incredible people from around the world. I pictured myself happy, confident and at peace finally. I spoke about my trip to anyone who would listen. I read travel guides, talked to friends who'd visited before and every night for around 9 months, honestly EVERY NIGHT without fail, I would watch Lord of the Rings. When I fell asleep, I dreamt of New Zealand.

I was **obsessed** with how I was going to save myself in New Zealand, and it happened.

I did climb mountains, I swam in the seas, I worked on several farms and met friends for life, plus I met my beautiful partner Yvonne. I am now happy, confident and at peace. I still bang on about New Zealand to anyone who will listen...

The magic of positive obsession is we begin to connect emotionally with the object of our obsessions. Before I'd even set foot in New Zealand, I'd imagined what would happen in vivid detail and with emotional intensity. I'd practised if you like, so much in my head, when it came to be there, I was ready to make it all happen.

Mind Movie Exercise

See your future life in front of you. Imagine it is 12 months from now and see what you will see, hear what you will hear and feel what you would feel. Make the images you see in your mind's eye big and bright, as if in high definition. Hear the sound in perfect quality. Invite the feelings you feel to double on your command. At the start of each day when you awake, keep your eyes closed and play this movie. Before going to sleep, play it again.

Reflections:

- How else can you become Obsessed with your vision?

Section Five

8 Principles for becoming Unstuck

Welcome to section 5 of the Book.

Another loving reminder before we dive into the 8 principles for becoming unstuck, what I've shared with you is totally useless... unless you apply it.

I can't say this enough. Information alone is useless.

A little about why I've chosen to share these 8 principles. As a self-proclaimed self-development nut, I'm fascinated to seek the answers to these questions...

Why is it some people change, and others stay

stuck?

Why is it some of us feel in charge of our lives and some of us feel helpless?

Based on my experience as a Coach and having got myself out of my very sticky situation in my early 20s, the way I see it, there are certain principles that when we adopt them, we have a better chance of successfully taking charge of their lives and becoming unstuck.

I know this list of 8 principles could be much longer.

There are heaps of helpful qualities and principles that can be applied to aid with feeling in control of our life.

In my eyes, these 8 are the *most* important principles.

Principle #1 Responsibility

No matter how much I protest, I am 100% responsible for what happens to me in my life.

- Dr Wayne Dyer

What Responsibility really means

Agree or disagree with this statement?

No matter how much I protest, I am 100% responsible for what happens to me in my life.

- Dr Wayne Dyer

Personally, I agree. Without a shadow of a doubt, we are all 100% responsible for what happens to us in our lives.

There is a chance you're thinking, "This is absurd, Will, how can we be 100% responsible for what happens to us in our lives? That means being responsible for *everything*, even all the terrible stuff that happens to us. What about trauma victims? What about the people in the world who lose their homes to natural disasters? What of those suffering from cancer?"

Now, if this sounds something like your train of thought, bear with me. I hear you, I really do.

Allow me to share with you my truth. Stepping into this new perspective just might change your world. Part of you may feel daunted, but part of you, I can almost guarantee, will feel liberated.

I first heard this statement about responsibility in 2016, during one of Dr Dyer's guided meditations on YouTube. I had really gotten into this particular guided meditation. It was an Ahhh meditation, requiring me to—you guessed it—Ahhh along out loud with Dr Dyer, and project this ancient sound out into the world.

There I sat each morning, alone on the cool and smooth tiles of my living room floor, Ahhh-ing away.

"Wow, I'm so spiritual, right now," I would think to myself, just before thinking, "That's not a very spiritual way of thinking, is it?"

Anyway, after about 10 minutes, Dr Dyer would introduce the second part of the guided meditation. In his distinctively deep voice, he would say, "We will now consider the affirmations of the day."

His affirmations resonated with me:

I know in each moment I am free to decide, and my past is nothing more than the trail I have left behind.

What drives my life today is the energy I generate in each of my present moments.

Naturally, my mind would commentate "Nice, so true, we are free to decide—and wow, you're on fire, Wayne, the past is nothing more than the trail I've left behind."

All of my mind's commentary sounded like

this, positive and in agreement. Well, almost all.

One affirmation just never sat right with me, and you may have guessed which affirmation this was:

No matter how much I protest, I am totally responsible for what happens to me in my life.

"Bullshit!" my mind would scream in protest.

"The other affirmations—faultless, Wayne, good job. I'm with you, mate. But this one…I'm not buying."

My attention now was torn away from the guided meditation, I would sit, embarrassed, as if a potty-mouthed friend had just barged in on my ultra-spiritual moment.

"Man, I was doing so well up until that point," I sulked.

Try as I might, every time I heard this affirmation, my reaction was the same. I just couldn't appreciate it—as far as I was concerned, it was wrong. It was as wrong as if Dr Dyer had been pointing at a white wall and telling me it was black.

Then, one day, the penny dropped.

I was listening to a podcast, and somebody was speaking about responsibility, they said this simple sentence:

"Responsibility literally means 'the ability to respond.'"

The cogs in my mind began to turn...

Hang on a minute, so what Dr Dyer is really saying is this: *no matter how much I protest, I am totally able to respond to what happens to me in my life.*

Boom. Yes, yes, a thousand times yes. I got it, finally.

This felt so different from my original train of thought.

The problem with the word responsibility is that it has become synonymous with the word blame.

"Who is responsible?" has evolved to "Who is to blame?" or "Whose fault is this?"

It was fascinating for me to observe the difference, emotionally, between viewing responsibility in these two lights.

When I viewed responsibility as being about blame, a strange cocktail of emotions came up: shame, shock, helplessness. I felt like a victim. However, now that I view responsibility as our ability to respond, well, I feel empowered, able, liberated. I feel like a victor, an owner of my fate.

Because isn't it true, no matter what life throws at us, that we are able to respond on some level?

We are able to respond by choosing what *meaning* we give to events—is this a problem or an opportunity? We are able to respond by *deciding* what actions we will take as a result of what happens to us—will I take on the role of a victim and do nothing, or will I take action and exercise my ability to respond?

You see, we totally have a choice. Not in what happens to us, but in how we use our ability to respond to what happens. In other words, we choose how responsible we want to be.

There are countless stories of humans in the most horrific of situations (Viktor Frankl, for example) who never forget their ability, or I would say power, to respond. No matter what life takes away from us, it will never take away our ability to respond.

Since the penny of understanding responsibility dropped, for me, life has been different. Now, when I'm faced with a challenge or an undesired situation, the first step I take is to remind myself that I am responsible for this.

I am responsible because this is the reality I have been served. Whether I asked for it or not, whether it was my fault or not, even whether I like it or not, this is my experience at this moment, and I feel powerful when I recognize my power to respond.

This Eckhart Tolle quote serves as a great reminder, as well: "Whatever the present moment contains, accept it as if you had chosen it. Always work with it, not against it."

Whatever happens to us between now and the rest of our lives, we are responsible.

Let's never forget the huge power we hold in our ability to respond.

Reflections:

- On a scale of 1-10 (with 10 being a high score), how responsible are you for your life right now?
- With a new understanding of the word responsible, how does this change things for you?

Principle #2 Acceptance

When you argue with reality, you lose, but only
100% of the time.

— Byron Katie

Here you go, Will

Imagine this scenario.

You have an important flight to catch in a few hours, you've invested several thousands of pounds in a week-long business retreat. You've booked a bus-transfer weeks in advance, as you leave the house you feel organized and excited for your trip away.

When you arrive at the bus stop, you stand alone with your luggage.

Glancing around, you feel surprised, you're the only soul waiting for the Bus.

10 minutes pass.

You're still alone and have the feeling something isn't right. It's partly the fact you seem to be the only person waiting at the bus stop, partly just a feeling you have.

You decide to pull out your bus ticket to double check the details. You read.

Your eyes grow wide in horror as your heart begins to sink into your stomach and a lump spawns in your throat. You realize the bus departed 90 minutes ago.

You've misread the arrival time at the airport and the departure time from the bus stop.

This was the last bus leaving for the airport this morning. Your heart beats faster and it feels like the blood surging in your veins has turned to ice.

"Rookie mistake", you think to yourself.

You walk over to the taxi rank, your only remaining option. An old lady wearing dark sunglasses winds down the window and you ask if she is free to drive you to the airport. She can, but it's not going to be cheap, you're a mistake is going to cost you dearly...

How would you be feeling at this point?

What thoughts would be going around your head?

This scenario was mine in October 2016.

A few days before this kerfuffle at the bus stop, I stumbled across the quote by Eckhart Tolle about accepting and working with reality and thought to myself, what an exciting and curious way of living it offers.

To simply accept what is. Not resisting, nor fighting the present moment.

How strange that only a few days later, the Universe would gift me with a perfect opportunity to test out this way of living. The Universe said "here you go, Will".

Let me be straight, my automatic response was a blend of anger, frustration and a pinch of panic. I wanted to play the blame game. I wanted to blame myself for being so stupid as to misread the timings. "You moron, a 4-year old can read better than you", the voice in my head would spit.

Alternatively, instead of beating myself up, I could choose to pass the buck and begin to blame the bus company for not making it clearer on the ticket. I could stew in my own soup of victimhood. (This always feels a bit better than mentally beating myself up).

These seem to be the 2 popular ways to deal with unwanted situations:

1. We blame ourselves for the situation by giving ourselves a hard time.

 or

2. We blame something outside of ourselves and give them a hard time.

But there is a third option. The road less travelled. One that doesn't involve any blaming and shaming.

3. Acceptance.

Simply accepting the present moment as it is and using our ability to respond.

Back to my story. I took a deep breath and I asked myself, how would I like to react?

What would acceptance look like? I'll be honest, I wanted to throw my toys out the pram, dive into the off-license for a pack of cigarettes and sulk, but another part of me was curious, I wondered if this whole acceptance thing was really possible. Because if you're anything like me, I often read an Idea and think to myself 'Yeah, great, that'll never work for me'. Which is funny because by believing this, it becomes a self-fulfilling prophecy and it won't work because we don't give it an opportunity to.

Back at the bus stop, with a smile on my face, I

smiled at the old lady taxi driver as I said Yes to her offer of driving me to the airport. I went to fetch the money from a nearby cash machine. It felt peculiar but at the same time, not forced. I genuinely felt at peace. My heartbeat was returning to normal, there was little tension in my body and much to my surprise, I wasn't in a bad mood either.

The taxi journey was, surprisingly pleasant. It took about 50 minutes to the airport through the beautiful winding roads of the German countryside over rolling hills and passing towering green forest. Inside the taxi, the old woman and I chatted like old friends the entire way as we learned about each other's lives, I thought I'd use the opportunity to practice my German. I got out the car and bid my new friend farewell. As she drove off, leaving me standing at the arrivals terminal, I felt calm and refreshed. The rest of the trip went smoothly, despite the unexpected start.

Now I'm not sharing this to pretend I'm some sort of Enlightened Guru (you know the type I mean).

I'm sharing this story to tell you, we always have a choice.

With awareness, we can choose to accept our reality, even in difficult, unpleasant and unwanted situations. I've continued to train myself to simply accept situations as they are and it's getting easier. When I've been ill, rather than resist and beat myself, through acceptance I've managed to respond kindly.

When personal mistakes or the mistakes of others have cost me time or money, I've accepted before responding as best I can.

Less Labels

For me, acceptance isn't about labelling what is, good or bad, which the mind loves to do, right?

This is good = I will feel good

This is crap = I will feel crap.

Acceptance is about playing with the cards that life has dealt you in each moment. It's entirely possible to be in a situation you haven't asked for and find undesirable and still accept it.

See for yourself, next time an unwanted situation pops up for you, see how you can control your reaction. Ask yourself the question, how would it look like if I were to respond in a way that serves me? Am I able to completely accept my current reality for what it is?

Something interesting happens when we respond to unwanted situations in a better way.

We show that often it's not the situation *itself* causing the stress and negativity, it's our *judgments and reaction* to the situation. In other words, it's our 'This should not be happening to me' thinking that is causing the stress.

But if I simply go around accepting everything

that happens, won't I become passive?

This is a great question that deserves a great answer. Nobody, I believe, can answer this question better than Byron Katie, author of a brilliant book titled *Loving What is* where she holds a similar philosophy of accepting our reality.

Her answer, I find brilliant.

"Surely it's better to accept reality as it is, than to fight and be in resistance with something that is a fact".

Of course, we do have a choice. We can choose to blame, resist what is true, tell ourselves the story that things should be different, but how does it serve us?

Acceptance for me is a bringer of Peace.

Accept and Trust Exercise

An exercise I like to do when I'm not feeling myself, a little down, lost or stressed, is to journal.

I grab my journal and pen and write our exactly how I'm feeling. At the top of the page, I create the heading ' I am feeling'... and fill the page with whatever comes up for me.

Once I feel I've captured how I'm feeling at that moment, at the bottom of the page I write the words "I accept this is how I feel and trust this will pass".

I believe the two most powerful words in any language are I am...

Because the words 'I am' are defining.

This is why in this exercise, I write I am feeling

instead of I am.

I am feeling... sends a different message to ourselves, it suggests there is a space between who we are and how we feel, which is absolutely true. We can never BE anxious or stressed, we can only experience the feelings of anxiety and stress.

We are the one experiencing the feelings, not the feelings themselves.

Reflections:

- Looking back over your life, what events do you need to accept have happened?

Principle # 3 Courage

Life is inherently risky.

There is only one big risk you should avoid at all costs, and that is the risk of doing nothing.

- Denis Waitley.

The Last holiday

A movie I adore is called "The Last Holiday" staring Queen Latifah.

If you haven't seen it, check it out. It's a real feel-good watch with an important message... **Live whilst you're alive!**

You see, the main character (played brilliantly by Queen Latifah) learns she is dying of an incurable brain tumour. Ouch. Rather than surrendering to her prognosis and waiting for her time to come, she shifts her life into fifth gear.

This woman finally quits the job she hates. She finally asks the man of her dreams out. She travels. Ok, I don't want to give too much of the movie plot away, but you get the picture! She lives!

Knowing her days were numbered, she connected with the courage inside of her and made things happen.

Allow me to throw a few questions at you.

What would you do if you found out you only had 1 year to live?

What impact would this knowledge have on your life?

How would you show up differently?

What would you prioritise? What would you let go of?

You need to know, I'm not asking this to make you fearful.

I'm asking you this question because the thing is... there are only two ultimate truths in life.

Firstly, we're all going to die.

Secondly, nobody can predict exactly when our time is up.

And I happen to believe, being mindful of these two truths can connect us with the courage we have inside of us.

Nowadays when I'm feeling fearful, I'll tell myself something along the lines of "Will, one day you're not going to be here mate and you won't have the opportunity. Life is short. Feel the fear, be courageous and do that scary thing right now boy!"

I can't tell you how many times I've given myself this talk during the process of writing this book because, you know, it's scary putting yourself and your words out there in the world.

No matter what your situation is right now, it's going to require courage for you to get unstuck and take charge of your life. Because by the time you've finished reading this book, it's going to be time for action. And even though you may be feeling super motivated and confident change is possible, you're going to be entering the realm of the New.

New thoughts. New decisions. New Actions. New habits. New environments. New feelings.

Which is going to require courage, because New is scary for the mind.

There will be moments your Gremlin pops up to plague you with fear and doubt. But you have to simply notice it and let it be. Remember your thoughts and your stories are not the real you. You are the endless power and potential experiencing the thoughts and ultimately you are the leader of your life.

Courage Muscle and the Fear Compass

Courage is a lot like a muscle, the more you use it the stronger it gets.

If you haven't flexed your courage muscle for a while, the thought of being courageous may be scary. The trick to growing stronger courage muscles, like training any muscle, is repetition.

Behaving courageously every day. Doing what scares you. Speaking your truth. Setting boundaries. Daring to go for what you want.

Begin to think of fear as a sign to move forward rather than move backwards.

Use Fear as a compass.

For a long time, I was terrified of doing a Facebook live. Imagining myself on live video in front of my family, friends, clients and followers was terrifying. I decided one day to commit to 7 days of Facebook lives in a row.

Day 1. Terrifying. Sweaty palms. Racing thoughts. Slurred speech. But I Gloria Gaynored... (I survived).

Day 7. Bearable.

Challenges like this are a brilliant way of growing our courage muscles.

Reflections:

- How might you create a challenge to grow your courage muscles?
- What scary decisions and actions have you been putting off?
- If you had limitless courage, what would you dare to ask for?

Principle # 4 Action

The time for action is now. It's never too late to do something.

- Antoine de Saint-Exupery

Will Aylward

The flaw with the law of Attraction

A book and movie that's done well over the last few years is *The Secret*.

If you haven't seen *The Secret*, I'll give you the general summary.

The Secret tells the stories of people who've used The Law of Attraction to achieve great success in life, business people, public speakers and authors who owe their success to "the secret'.

The Law of Attraction is the idea that we attract in life what we think about. Simply put: Think negatively and negative things will happen, think positively and positive things will happen.

I'm not going to go into my personal thoughts about The Secret or the Law of Attraction. But what I will say is this...

The movie does not emphasise **action** enough.

I know of people who've seen the movie and tell themselves "If I just think about what I want, if I just think positively, I'll get what I want."

If this was true, we'd all be super fit, successful and happy, just by thinking about being fit, successful and happy.

Positive thinking is good but it's not enough.

We need to take action.

Creating a forest one seed at a time

There once was a man who lived in the Scottish Highlands.

He lived happily alone until he died of old age. He was a very active man, as each day he would have to walk a fair distance across the hills to the village where he worked.

Something special happened during this walk.

The man had a ritual.

For as long as he could remember, he planted a single seed.

Just one, tiny, seed, buried into the earth.

He did this every day, without fail.

By the time the man passed, the land on the hills had transformed beyond recognition.

The man had created an entire Forest.

This is one of my favourite short stories.

It reminds me I'm powerful. I'm powerful because like the man in the story, and like you, I always have the ability to take action. We all do!

Right now, if you wanted to, you could stop reading this book and take action. I hope you don't though, keep reading...

The 4 levels of Action

Never reduce a target. Instead, increase actions
- Grant Cardone.

A book I revisit time and time again is The 10X Rule by Grant Cardone. I have the audiobook version because I like his enthusiastic energy and accent. Plus, as much as I adore reading a real-life book, I find audiobooks are easy to consume when on the go.

One of my biggest takeaways from The 10X Rule is the 4 levels of Action.

When I find myself feeling stuck in a rut, I ask myself what level of action I'm operation at. It'll be helpful for you too, to do the same.

Level 1: No Action.

 Level 2: Retreating Action.

Taking little actions but still retreating from the big and important actions because of fear.

Level 3: Normal levels of action. Doing enough, taking average amounts of action.

Level 4: Massive levels of Action.

Taking more action than needed.

My philosophy is this.

There's absolutely a time for rest, recovery and recreation.

My least favourite word is *hustle*. Nothing is cool about being burnt out and doing too much. But, and this is important but, there are times we need to take action, times we need to get out there and plant seeds, and lots of them.

The bottom line is this. To feel in charge and become unstuck, action is required.

What a tick bite taught me about working smart

Last summer I took a run in the Forest.

To cool off, I took a shower and as I was lathering myself up, I soon realized I wasn't showering alone. Nestled deep within the top of my leg, an inch or two below my bum was a deer tick.

Following its painful removal after a visit to the Emergency Doctor, I was prescribed a two-week course of antibiotics to prevent me from developing Lyme Disease.

The anti-biotics kicked my arse.

Within 20 minutes of taking my first round, I was in the deepest sleep.

I was a zombie for the next 3 weeks.

It was near impossible to concentrate, my eyes constantly felt heavy and my stomach was iffy.

Running my Coaching business was going to prove difficult. Indeed.

I had about 3 and a half hours each day when I felt human.

I quickly became aware that if I was to keep progressing over the next 3 weeks, I would have to work smart and ensure I'm doing the *most important* tasks each day.

Each morning I was sat at my desk, journal in front of me, pen in hand, answering the following question.

"What are the actions, that if I took them today, would progress me forward most towards my goals"?

They were a tough 3 weeks, but I got by because I worked smart.

Taking action is essential but that's not to say we have to become busy fools in the process of achieving our goals.

It's easy to get lost in all the possible actions we could take.

We live in a world of endless possibilities.

Focus on your *most important actions* and take them.

Reflections:

- What level of action are you currently operating at?
- Thinking of your Vision/Goals, what are the most important steps you need to take?

Principle # 5 Trust

Trust.

Middle English: from the Old Norse 'traust' meaning strong.

With Trust comes Strength

Isn't that exactly how we feel when we place our trust in someone or something? Strong.

Another key principle to becoming unstuck is... Trust.

Because if we don't Trust, we doubt, and when we live life from a place of doubt, not a lot happens. Other than procrastination and over-thinking, which make us feel like we're doing something, except we're not really.

The Story of the Farmer's Son

Many years ago, there lived an old farmer.

One day he woke up to find all of his horses had escaped their paddocks and ran away.

Upon hearing the news his neighbour of many years said "That's bad isn't it"?

The farmer replied "Good or bad, hard to say."

The next day whilst out in the fields, the farmer and his son looked out to the horizon and what did they see? Their horses returning, but they weren't alone. They were galloping along with 12 new wild horses.

The neighbour, walking over and seeing the horses for himself, exclaimed, "Oh boy, that's good, isn't it!"

The farmer replied "Good or bad, hard to say."

The next day, whilst attempting to train one of the wild horses, the Farmer's son fell and broke his arm badly.

The neighbour, shaking his head said "That's

bad isn't it."

Once again, the farmer replied "Good or bad, hard to say."

A week or so later, the farmer received a knock on the door. He'd barely had a chance to open the door before two, great, big soldiers burst in and demanded all fit young men of fighting age go with them immediately, to join the war against their enemies. Seeing the farmer's son whose arm was in a sling, they spared him and left just as abruptly as they have arrived.

The neighbour peeked his head through the window (having been secretly watching the whole ordeal) whispered, "Phew, that's good isn't it!"

Once again, the old farmer replied "Good or bad, hard to say."

In this story, the farmer had trust. He accepted

reality as it was, without labelling his reality as good or bad, unlike his neighbour.

The farmer *trusted* life was happening for him, not to him.

This is a hugely important distinction.

When I was stuck, I felt life was happening *to* me. I realise now, it was happening *for* me. At the very start I told you:

- I was frustrated and stuck in an unfulfilling Insurance job.

- I was hopelessly single, stuck in the 'Friend Zone'.

- I was overweight and unfit, living on junk-food, the only exercise I got was a walk to the Kebab shop.

- I was massively anxious and would run into the toilet at work to have panic attacks, throwing water on my face to calm myself down.

- I had rock bottom confidence and self-esteem (which I over-compensated for by playing a Jack-the-lad role).

- I partied to numb the pain, partying Thursday through to Sunday, drinking enough Guinness to kill a small horse and smoking like a sailor.

- I was in increasing debt with 3 payday loan companies, struggling to make the repayments each month.

Looking back, all of my (what I viewed at the time as) problems, were secretly opportunities. They were given to me, I don't know by whom, maybe God, the Universe, who knows. But they were given to me and happening for me.

- My job frustration happened for me to guide me towards discovering my true purpose.

- My hopelessly single time taught me the importance of loving myself first!

- My poor health and fitness happened for me as in the process of getting back in shape, I gained a wealth of health and fitness knowledge.

- My low confidence happened for me because whilst re-connecting with my confidence, I discovered I could do more than the voice in my head told me I could.

- My partying to numb the pain, well it was great fun! Haha, no seriously. I formed some great friendships in my partying days.

- My money troubles happened for me because they forced me to learn the value of money and take responsibility for my finances.

The way I see it, my situation only got better when I became aware no one was going to come and save me and until I learned the lessons I needed to learn, the problems were going to keep popping up time and time again.

Reflections:

- What are the hidden opportunities in your current problems?
- What are the potential lessons you need to learn?

Doubt the Doubt

Begin to Doubt your Doubts!

So often we don't challenge our doubts in life, which only reinforces the notion they must be true. Use the power of doubt in a way that serves you and doubt your doubts.

Trust the past has happened for you, not to you.

Trust in your capability in becoming unstuck, starting right now.

Trust your vision for the future is possible.

Principle # 6 Decision

You are not the victim of the world, but rather the master of your own destiny. It is your choices and decisions that determine your destiny.

— Roy T. Bennett

Don't be an Indecisive Donkey

Did you hear the story about the donkey who died of indecision?

The donkey stood in the middle of his stable.

To his left, a few metres away lay a fresh bale of straw.

To his right, also a few metres away, stood a trough full of water.

The donkey thought to himself "Should I eat, or should I drink"?

He took a few steps towards the bale of straw. He stopped. Turned. Walked a few steps towards the water. Stopped. Turned around and walked back towards the bale of straw.

The donkey could not make his mind up and

this continued for several days... before he died.

The story demonstrates an important truth... not deciding is a decision itself and will come with its own results.

Meaning, making decisions - good decisions - is essential for saving ourselves and taking charge of our lives. Where you are right now, reading this book, has happened because, at some point, you made the decision to do so.

In fact, in a single day, it's estimated we make (hold-on-to-your-hat) 35,000 conscious decisions. That's a lot of decisions daily.

So how can we make better decisions?

Making Decisions right

So often, we stay stuck in indecision because we focus so much on making the "right decision". Let's be honest, unless you have psychic abilities, it's impossible to know 100% right now what the "right decision" is. Although we may have a strong gut feeling, so often in life, only time will tell (think back to the story of the farmer).

Instead, we can decide to focus on making a decision right.

Meaning, once we've decided, through action, persistence and remembering our ability to respond, we do our absolute best to create the outcome we want. Of course, through focusing on what is in our control, compared to what isn't.

This powerful little switch from *making-the-right-decision* to *making-the-decision-right* feels so different. Rather than pressured, we can feel empowered, knowing our ability to make decisions and take actions is infinite.

Make another one

Remember you can make an infinite number of decisions.

My wonderful friend and fellow Coach, Yolande Olhaus-Sluiter, once shared some of her wisdom, "you can always make another decision."

When at the crossroads of making a decision, it can be easy to forget this important truth.

It's rare in life that if we felt we've made the wrong decision, it's irreversible.

As I once told a friend who was anxious about travelling "Don't forget if you get there and hate it, you can always decide to come home".

Decide and then Act

As the story of the Ducks on the Log demonstrated earlier on, a real decision is always followed by some form of action.

Get into the habit of taking actions, even if it's a tiny action, once you've made a decision.

Reflections:

- What decisions have you been putting off lately and what are you going to do about it?

- If you were to focus on making decisions right instead of the right decisions, what difference would this make?

Principle # 7 Permission

Have you given yourself Permission to feel, be, do, and have all you want in life?

No more permission slips

Do you remember your school days?

Remember the old permission slips we would have to take home and have signed to allow us on school trips? Our parents or guardians were required to give their signature to confirm we children had been given permission to visit the Zoo.

No permission slip = No school trip.

I'll assume your school days are over and you're a legal adult in your country of residence when I say this...

The only person who can give you permission in life now is **you**.

You are in charge.

Often after a client shares their vision with me, I'll ask them "Have you given yourself permission to have that?"

It's often the first time they've considered the question.

They start to think "How do I know if I've given myself permission or not"?

The answer is simple. We know when we've given ourselves permission to have what we really want when we place *no barriers* up to receiving.

You see, most people limit the amount of happiness, success and money they allow themselves. Often out of fear of disapproval for appearing greedy but, more commonly I believe, out of not feeling worthy enough.

The Gremlin in our heads asks "Who am I to be so happy"?

"Who am I to be so successful"? "Who am I to have such financial abundance"?

I ask the opposite, who are you NOT to?

You, as much as anybody else in the world, deserves to be happy and enjoy the abundance life has to offer. Drop any stories that say you're somehow not worthy or not good enough.

You are, you always have been, and you always will be worthy!

Reflections:

- What if the only real obstacle that could stop you from creating the life of your dreams is a lack of permission from yourself?
- If you gave yourself total and absolute permission to live life your way, what would that look like?

Principle # 8 Self-Love

You yourself as much as anybody in the Universe, deserves your love and affection.

- Buddha.

Make self-love the motivation, not shame

The notion of Self-Love used to make my skin crawl with cringy-ness.

I had learned its "normal" to constantly doubt and criticise myself and anyone who thought Self-Love was a good idea was just a deluded hippy.

Nothing could be further from the truth.

If you're lucky enough to have young children in your life, you'll know how loving they are towards themselves. They allow themselves joy through constant play and place no limits on the amount of love they receive, because they know they are worthy of love and happiness. They haven't yet learned how to give themselves a hard time or think critical thoughts.

This is our true nature. To truly make lasting change, Self-Love needs to be the motivation.

An unshakeable belief in our own self-worth.

I mean, have you ever tried to shame yourself into changing?

How did that work out for you?

This is a popular -yet faulted- strategy for trying to motivate ourselves to change. The thinking of "If I just give myself a hard-enough time, tell myself I'm; useless/fat/boring/not good enough/lazy, enough times then eventually I'll have to change."

Try Kindness. Try Compassion. Try loving yourself.

Take care of yourself like you would take care of a small child. Love yourself more than you feel is necessary, more than feels comfortable, and see what happens.

What would Love do?

I once worked with a client who underwent an amazing transformation.

We worked together for 12 months and would have a Call every 2 weeks.

When we started working together, she constantly had self-critical and self-doubting thoughts and as a result, she lived in a state of worry and panic.

Today, I'm pleased to say she is a very different woman. Practising self-love has been a *huge* part of her success.

Each morning, she creates a little time for herself to meditate and do some yoga.

Out of love for herself, she has created boundaries with those around her. She has stopped saying Yes when she's rather say no.

She's given herself permission to have the life she wants and has achieved goals that 12 months ago seemed impossible.

She eats healthier foods because she enjoys taking care of herself.

At the end of one of our calls, she said "Will, I feel like I've returned home to myself."

I didn't have to ask her what she meant by this. I could see the sparkle in her eyes.

Self-Love was at the core of my client's transformation.

One change to make right now, stop being so hard on yourself.

Reflections:

- If you were to score your level of Self-Love out of 10 (10 being high) what would you score it at?

- What would a 10 look like?

Over to you

In a moment, once the final page of this book has been turned, the last of its words read, it's over to you.

You'll be faced with a choice.

A choice we face in every given moment, to do what we've always done and walk the safe, familiar paths we know, or to walk a different path, a new path. A path where your exciting Vision for the future pulls you forward, a path where you take action despite not feeling 100% ready or motivated, a path where you leave the old limiting beliefs and stories of the past in the past.

There are many others books out there that will help you to walk your desired path and there are certainly people who can help pick you up when you fall down. But you, and only you, can do the walking.

A final question

When I was a kid, I loved to write poetry. I used to arrive at primary school 20 minutes early, my scruffy scrapbook in hand to show my latest creations with my teachers.

Anyways, a couple of years ago, I was working with a Coach who encouraged me to rekindle my love of writing poetry and writing. In fact, without him, I doubt this book would be written. Thank you, Tim Mikelj.

This poem is called If Only and is written from the perspective of an old man reflecting on his life as death draws near.

If Only

If only I had a little more time, A couple more chapters, a few more lines.

I'm on the final page, lying almost dead, looking over my life- in this Hospital Bed.

If I could rewrite, if a second chance given, I'd make the most of my second time living.

I'd take care of myself: my body and mind, learn to relax, learn to be kind.

I'd let go of the past, let old chapters be, look back only for lessons that the tough times taught me.

I'd make time daily- to laugh, dance and sing, and bathe in the joy and love that they bring.

I'd be who I am, not as I 'should' be, A true, authentic, version of me.

Speak my truth, even when my voice starts to shake, be real and imperfect, not perfect and fake.

Spend more time with my parents, my wife and my girls, they wanted my love, not promises and pearls.

I'd slow each moment down, stopping the hurry, feeling each breath, exhaling all worry

I'd explore the Earth, Berlin to Beijing, instead of stuffing my house with thing after thing.

I'd take risks in pursuit of chasing my dreams, the risk is rarely as big as it seems.

But now it's too late, my regrets die with me.

At the end of your life,

what will your story be?

About the Author

Will Aylward is a Life Coach for Ambitious Professionals and Entrepreneurs and believes the key to Joy and Success in life is Courage. Becoming Unstuck is his first published book and he intends to write many more.

Will lives in Germany's oldest City, Trier with his partner Yvonne where he spends his time Coaching, running in the Forest, playing the piano and people watching over a fine Espresso.

You may find out more about him, enjoy his blogs and more free stuff over at www.willaylward.com

Printed in Poland
by Amazon Fulfillment
Poland Sp. z o.o., Wrocław